Scott Foresman - Addison Wesley
MIDDLE SCHOOL MATH

Problem-Solving Workbook
For Guided Problem Solving

Course 1

Scott Foresman - Addison Wesley

Editorial Offices: Menlo Park, California • Glenview, Illinois
Sales Offices: Reading, Massachusetts • Atlanta, Georgia • Glenview, Illinois
Carrollton, Texas • Menlo Park, California

http://www.sf.aw.com

ISBN 0–201–31807-5

Copyright © Addison Wesley Longman, Inc.

Printed in the United States of America

5 6 7 8 9 10 – BW – 02 01 00 99

Contents

Chapter 10: Ratio, Proportion, and Percent

Chapter 11: Solids and Measurement

Chapter 12: Probability

Overview

The *Problem-Solving Workbook* (For Guided Problem Solving) provide a step-by-step approach to solve a problem selected from the student book. These selections are made from the *Practice and Apply* section or from the *Problem Solving and Reasoning* section. Some of these selections are routine in nature and cover basic concepts. Others are nonroutine and might involve multiple-step problems, problems with too much information, problems involving critical thinking, and so on. An icon in the Teacher's Edition flags the selected problem so that the teacher will know what problem is provided on each worksheet.

How to use

The Problem-Solving Worksheets are designed so that the teacher can use them in many different ways:

a. As a teaching tool to guide students in exploring and mastering a specific problem-solving skill or strategy. Making a transparency of the worksheet provides an excellent way to expedite this process as students work along with the teacher at their desks.

b. As additional practice in solving problems for students who have had difficulty in completing the assignment.

c. As independent or group work to help students reach a better understanding of the problem-solving process.

d. As a homework assignment that may encourage students to involve their parents in the educational process.

Description of the master

The problem to be solved is stated at the top of each worksheet. The worksheet is then divided into the four steps of the Problem-Solving Guidelines that are used throughout the student text. Each step includes key questions designed to guide students through the problem-solving process. At the bottom of each worksheet, *Solve Another Problem* allows students to use their skills to solve a problem similar to the original problem. This helps reinforce the problem-solving skills and strategies they have just used in solving the problem on the worksheet.

The Guided Problem Solving worksheet on the next page can be used as a guide to help students organize their work as they complete the *Solve Another Problem.* It may also be used to assist students in solving any problem as they complete the four steps of the Problem-Solving Guidelines.

1. **Understand** ensures that students are able to interpret the problem and determine key facts.

2. **Plan** actively involves students in devising a plan or strategy for solving the problem. They may be asked to choose a fact or formula that could be used to solve the problem. In other cases, students may be asked to model the problem or draw a picture. Other times, students will be asked to choose a strategy they can use to solve the problem. Problem-solving strategies often used include: Look for a Pattern, Make a Table, Work Backward, Draw a Diagram, Make an Organized List, Guess and Check, Use Logical Reasoning, and Solve a Simpler Problem.

3. **Solve** encourages students to carry out the plan and arrive at an answer. Students may be asked to answer the question using a full sentence.

4. **Look Back** encourages students to review their work and check their answer to see if it is reasonable. This step often asks students to reflect on the strategy they used or to suggest other strategies they could also have used to solve the problem. It is important that students think of this step as a natural part of the problem-solving process.

Name _____

— Understand —

— Plan —

— Solve —

— Look Back —

Ocean sizes are often measured in square miles. Use this measurement and the graph to answer the question.

The total area of the Pacific, Atlantic, and Indian Oceans is 124,000,000 square miles. How many square miles is the Pacific Ocean?

Ocean Sizes

Atlantic ⬤⬤⬤⬤⬤⬤⬤⬤

Indian ⬤⬤⬤⬤⬤⬤⬤

Arctic ⬤◗

Key ⬤ = 4,000,000 sq. mi

▬ Understand ▬

1. What does the problem ask you to find?

_____

2. Which oceans have a combined area of 124,000,000 square miles?

_____

▬ Plan ▬

3. Use the graph. What is the area of

a. the Atlantic Ocean? _____   **b.** the Indian Ocean? _____

4. What is the combined area of the Atlantic and Indian Oceans? _____

▬ Solve ▬

5. Write a number sentence to find the area of the Pacific Ocean.

_____

6. What is the area of the Pacific Ocean? _____

▬ Look Back ▬

7. How can you use addition to check your answer?

_____

_____

SOLVE ANOTHER PROBLEM

The total area of the Arctic and Indian Oceans, and the South China Sea is 35,000,000 square miles.

How many square miles is the South China Sea? _____

Name _____

Use the population graph.
How many more 5–13 year-olds will there
be in the year 2000 than there were in the
year when their population was the smallest?

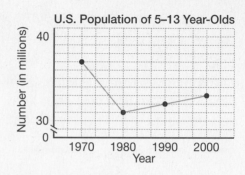

U.S. Population of 5–13 Year-Olds

▬ Understand ▬

1. Circle the question.

2. How do you find the number of 5–13 year-olds for 1970?

_____

_____

3. What does the jagged line represent on the vertical scale?

_____

▬ Plan ▬

4. What year was the population of 5–13 year-olds the smallest? _____

5. How many 5–13 year-olds were there in
the year the population was the smallest? _____

6. How many 5–13 year-olds
will there be in the year 2000? _____

▬ Solve ▬

7. Choose the number sentence you will use to solve the problem. _____

a. 33 + 31 = 64   **b.** 33 − 31 = 2   **c.** 37 − 31 = 6

8. Write your answer in a complete sentence.

_____

▬ Look Back ▬

9. How could you have solved the problem in another way?

_____

_____

SOLVE ANOTHER PROBLEM

How many more 5–13 year-olds were
there in the year 1990 than in the year 1980? _____

Name _____

Use the Calorie Requirements graph.
At what age is the difference in
calorie needs the greatest between
males and females? The smallest?
How can you tell?

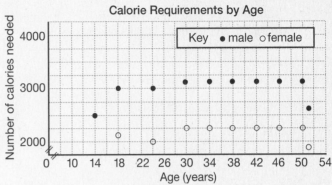

━━ Understand ━━

1. What do these points represent?

     a. solid _____

     b. open _____

2. What does the distance between two points at any age represent?

_____

_____

━━ Plan ━━

3. The greatest distance between two points for any age is at age _____.

4. The smallest distance between two points for any age is at age _____.

━━ Solve ━━

5. At what age is the difference in calorie needs the greatest between

     males and females? How can you tell? _____

_____

6. At what age is the difference in calorie needs the smallest between

     males and females? How can you tell? _____

_____

━━ Look Back ━━

7. How can you use subtraction to verify your answer? _____

_____

_____

SOLVE ANOTHER PROBLEM

At what ages is the difference in calorie needs about the same? _____

Draw a line plot of the ages of the first ten Presidents when they took office.

Age of First Ten Presidents

Age	Frequency
49	1
54	1
57	4
58	1
61	2
68	1

━ Understand ━

1. What are you asked to do?

_____

_____

2. What mark do you use to record an item of data on a line plot? _____

━ Plan ━

3. List the President's ages. _____

4. The smallest number you record is _____.

5. The largest number you record is _____.

6. How many marks will you write for one President's age? _____

━ Solve ━

7. Write the ages in order from youngest to oldest on the line plot. Include all ages between the youngest and oldest.

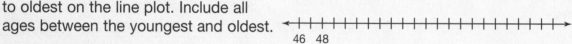

46 48

8. Record the data.

━ Look Back ━

9. How can you make sure that you have recorded each data item in the line plot? _____

_____

SOLVE ANOTHER PROBLEM

Make a line plot to represent the value of the coins in this data set: dime, nickel, dime, penny, nickel, penny, dime, dime, penny, nickel, nickel, penny, penny, dime, dime, nickel, penny, nickel, dime, dime

Jarvis made a four-digit number with 0, 3, 6, and 8. The number was smaller than 5 but bigger than 1. What could his number be? Explain.

⬛ Understand ⬛

1. How many digits will there be in Jarvis's number? _____

2. Underline the clue that helps you find the first digit.

⬛ Plan ⬛

3. Is Jarvis's number a whole number or a decimal? Explain.

_____

_____

⬛ Solve ⬛

4. Write the first digit of one number made from 0, 3, 6, and 8 in the first box at the right. Explain how you know.

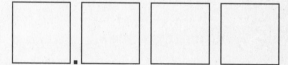

_____

5. Write the remaining digits in as many ways as you can.

_____

6. Look at each way you listed the digits in Item 5. Does the order of the remaining three digits make any difference in whether the number is less than 5 or greater than 1? Explain.

_____

_____

⬛ Look Back ⬛

7. What strategy can you use to make sure that you have listed all the possible numbers that meet the criteria?

_____

_____

SOLVE ANOTHER PROBLEM

Agatha made a five-digit number with 0, 3, 5, 8, and 9. The number is bigger than 39 and smaller than 53. The thousandths digit is 3 times the tenths digit. What number did Agatha make? _____

Wendell and Terry both rounded the number 3.4682. Wendell says that he rounded the number up. Terry says that he rounded the number down. To what place value might the number have been rounded by Wendell? By Terry? Explain.

━━ Understand ━━

1. Underline the information that you need.

━━ Plan ━━

2. When is a number rounded up? _____

_____

━━ Solve ━━

3. Would you round each number up or down when rounding to the

a. ones place? _____   **b.** tenths place? _____

c. hundredths place? _____   **d.** thousandths place? _____

4. Wendell rounded up. List all the place values that the number might have been rounded to by Wendell. Explain.

_____

5. Terry rounded down. List all the place values that the number might have been rounded to by Terry. Explain.

_____

━━ Look Back ━━

6. Why didn't you check ten-thousandths as a place value?

_____

SOLVE ANOTHER PROBLEM

Casey and Jenna both rounded the number 42.185. Casey rounded the number up. Jenna rounded the number down. To what place value might the number have been rounded by Casey? By Jenna? Explain.

_____

_____

© Scott Foresman Addison Wesley 6

The chart shows the finishing times for a swimming race. Who came in first, second, and third?

Swimmer	Time (sec)
Gabe	32.01
Raul	31.84
Josh	31.92

━ Understand ━

1. How long did it take Raul to finish the race? _____

2. Is the fastest time less than or greater than the slowest time? Explain.

_____

_____

━ Plan ━

3. To list the times in order, which digits will you compare first? _____

Second? _____ Third? _____ Fourth? _____

━ Solve ━

4. Write the times in order from least to greatest. _____

5. Write the times in order from fastest to slowest. _____

6. Who came in first? _____ Second? _____ Third? _____

━ Look Back ━

7. Did you need to compare all the place values to order the times? Explain.

_____

_____

SOLVE ANOTHER PROBLEM

The chart shows the finishing times for a relay race. Who came in first, second, and third?

_____

Runner	Time (sec)
Lynn	28.10
Kenisha	28.01
Raylene	21.08

In 1993, the U.S. Post Office released a large number of stamps picturing Elvis Presley. In scientific notation, the exponent is 8. The decimal factor has three digits, all of them odd. It's greater than 5.13, less than 5.19, and all the digits are different. How many Elvis Presley stamps were issued in 1993?

━━ Understand ━━

1. What are you asked to find? _____

_____

2. How will the number of stamps be written? _____

   a. Standard notation   **b.** Scientific notation

━━ Plan ━━

3. Write the power of ten for the number of stamps. _____

4. The digits in the decimal factor are odd.
Which digits could be in the decimal factor? _____

5. The decimal factor is between 5.13 and 5.19. Which digit is

   a. in the ones place? _____   **b.** in the tenths place? _____

   c. Since no digit can be repeated in the answer,
   which digit can be used in the hundredths place? _____

━━ Solve ━━

6. Combine the information you found in Items 4 and 5 to write a sentence stating how many Elvis stamps were issued in 1993.

_____

_____

━━ Look Back ━━

7. Which strategy did you use to find your answer? _____

┌─────────────────────────────────────┐
│ **SOLVE ANOTHER PROBLEM** │
└─────────────────────────────────────┘

A number in scientific notation uses only digits that are multiples of 3, except for the base of 10 in the power of ten. Each digit is used once and the number is the largest number possible. What is the number?

_____

You bought four pairs of pants at the same price. Based on rounding, your estimate of the total cost was $40 before tax.

a. If you rounded to the nearest dollar, what is the maximum price for each pair? Explain.

b. If you rounded to the nearest dollar, what is the minimum price? Explain.

▬ Understand ▬

1. Underline the information you need.

2. To estimate, you will round to the nearest _____.

▬ Plan ▬

3. Each pair of pants costs the same amount.
What is the estimated cost of each pair of pants? _____

4. To find the maximum price, will you look for a number that rounds up or rounds down to 10? Explain. _____

_____

▬ Solve ▬

5. What is the maximum price for each pair of pants? _____

6. What is the minimum price for each pair of pants? _____

▬ Look Back ▬

7. Write number sentences to check your answers. _____

_____

SOLVE ANOTHER PROBLEM

You bought three CDs at the same price. Based on rounding, your estimate of the total cost was $36 before tax. If you rounded to the nearest dollar, what is the maximum price for each CD? What is the minimum price? Explain your answers.

_____

_____

Name _____

One day, 1 Japanese yen was worth 0.0098 U.S. dollars.
The same day, a Swedish krona was worth 0.1297 U.S. dollars.

a. How much more was the krona worth than the yen that day?

b. On the same day, 1 Thai baht was worth 0.0398 U.S. dollars. How much U.S. money equals one baht plus one yen?

▬ Understand ▬

1. How many U.S. dollars was one Japanese yen worth? _____

2. How many U.S. dollars was one Swedish krona worth? _____

3. How many U.S. dollars was one Thai baht worth? _____

▬ Plan ▬

4. Which operation will you use to find how much more one currency is than another? _____

5. Which operation will you use to find how much two currencies are worth together? _____

▬ Solve ▬

6. How much more was the krona worth than the yen? Compare in U.S. dollars. _____

7. How many U.S. dollars equal one baht plus one yen? _____

▬ Look Back ▬

8. Would a grid model help you find the answer? Explain.

_____

_____

| **SOLVE ANOTHER PROBLEM** |

One day, 1 Canadian dollar was worth 0.7319 U.S. dollars. The same day, a German mark was worth 0.6430 U.S. dollars.

a. How much more was the Canadian dollar worth than the German mark that day? _____

b. On the same day, 1 Pakistani rupee was worth 0.0252 U.S. dollars. How much U.S. money equals one mark plus one rupee? _____

Jorge won a cash prize in a contest. He donated half of the money to his Boy Scout troop. Then he spent $19.49 on a computer game and put the rest, $30.51 into his savings account. How much money did he win?

━━ Understand ━━

1. What are you asked to find? _____

2. What was the first thing Jorge did with his winnings? _____

_____

3. What were the second and third things Jorge did with his winnings? _____

_____

_____

━━ Plan ━━

4. Which strategy will you use to find the answer? _____

    a. Work Backward   **b.** Look for a Pattern   **c.** Make a Table

5. Jorge donated half of his winnings to the Boy Scouts. What fraction did he spend on other things? _____

6. What is the first operation you will use? _____

━━ Solve ━━

7. How much money did Jorge have before he bought the game? _____

8. How much did Jorge win in the contest? _____

━━ Look Back ━━

9. What other strategies could you use to find the answer? _____

_____

_____

SOLVE ANOTHER PROBLEM

Hector received some cash for his birthday. He spent $14.30 on a CD and donated $25.00 to a charity. He put half of what was left into his savings account. He has $17.85 left. How much money did he receive on his birthday? _____

Andrea drinks 54.3 ounces of milk every week. She also drinks a 6-ounce can of orange juice and 8 glasses of water every day. If she drinks 544.3 ounces of liquid in a week and every glass of water is the same size, how big is each glass of water?

━ Understand ━

1. What are you asked to find? _____

2. Circle the data given in ounces per week.

3. Underline the data given in ounces per day.

━ Plan ━

4. How will you find how much Andrea drinks in one week when you are given the amount she drinks each day? _____

5. How many glasses of water does she drink each day? _____

6. How many glasses of water does she drink each week? _____

7. How many ounces of orange juice does she drink each week? _____

━ Solve ━

8. How many ounces of milk and juice does she drink each week? _____

9. Subtract to find how many ounces of water she drinks each week. _____

10. Divide by 56 to find how many ounces each glass of water holds. _____

━ Look Back ━

11. How can you work backward to check your answer? _____

_____

_____

SOLVE ANOTHER PROBLEM

Kelsey earns $65.30 every week working at a grocery store and $5 every day walking a neighbor's dog. She also watches her brother for 2 hours every day. If she earns $128.30 each week, how much does she earn each hour she watches her brother? _____

Estimate first. Then solve.

In 1863, emigrants could buy rice for $0.11 per pound in Chimney Rock, Nebraska. The Wilson's barrel could hold 19.25 pounds. How much did it cost to fill the barrel?

▬ Understand ▬

1. Circle the information you need.

▬ Plan ▬

2. Which operation will you use to find the cost to fill the barrel? _____

3. Estimate your answer by rounding.

    a. Round $0.11 to the nearest tenth. _____

    b. Round $19.25 to the nearest ten. _____

▬ Solve ▬

4. Use your rounded numbers to estimate the cost. _____

5. Find the actual cost to fill the barrel.
Round your answer to the nearest cent. _____

▬ Look Back ▬

6. How can you tell if your answer is reasonable?

_____

_____

7. Why did you have to round your answer to Item 5?

_____

_____

SOLVE ANOTHER PROBLEM

Estimate first. Then solve.

In 1996, brown rice cost $1.09 per pound. How much would it cost the Wilsons to fill their 19.25-pound barrel with rice in 1996?

_____

Name _____

In a gymnastic competition, Dominique scored 9.5, 9.6, 9.5, 9.4, 9.7, and 9.6. Kim scored 9.5, 9.4, 9.6, 9.7, 9.7, and 9.5. Who had the higher average score? Explain.

Understand

1. Circle Dominique's scores.

2. Underline Kim's scores.

3. How many scores did each girl receive? _____

Plan

4. How do you find the average score? _____

_____

Solve

5. How many points did each girl score in all?

   a. Dominique _____   **b.** Kim _____

6. What was each girl's average score?

   a. Dominique _____   **b.** Kim _____

7. Who had the higher average score? Explain. _____

_____

Look Back

8. How could you find who had the higher average without doing all the calculations? _____

_____

_____

SOLVE ANOTHER PROBLEM

In an ice skating competition, Alex scored 7.2, 7.5, 7.1, 6.9, and 7.7. Mario scored 7.1, 7.5, 7.8, 7.0, and 6.9. Who had the higher average score? Explain.

_____

Manuel was counting the lights on parade floats. Each float was 36.4 feet long, and they ran bumper to bumper for 5314.4 feet. If there were 150 lights on each float, how many lights did he count?

━ Understand ━

1. What are you asked to find? _____

2. Underline the information you need.

━ Plan ━

3. How can you find how many floats were in the parade? _____

_____

4. Given the number of floats, how can you find the number of lights?

_____

_____

━ Solve ━

5. Write equations showing the number of floats and lights on floats in the parade.

   a. Floats _____   **b.** Lights _____

6. How many lights did Manuel count? _____

━ Look Back ━

7. How could you use the strategy, Solve a Simpler Problem, to find the number of lights? _____

_____

_____

SOLVE ANOTHER PROBLEM

Cybill was counting the lights on her neighbor's fence. Each section of the fence was 6.2 feet long, and the fence was 210.8 feet long. If there were 25 lights on each section, how many lights did she count?

_____

A wagon weighs 165.3 kg. Carrying riders, the wagon weighs 465 kg.
What is the weight of the riders?

▬ Understand ▬

1. How much does the empty wagon weigh? _____

2. How much does the wagon with riders weigh? _____

▬ Plan ▬

3. Which operation will you use to find the weight of the riders? _____

4. Which number sentence would be a
   good estimate for the weight of the riders? _____

   a. 500 − 200 = 300   **b.** 500 × 200 = 1000   **c.** 500 + 200 = 700

▬ Solve ▬

5. How much more does the wagon
   carrying riders weigh than the empty wagon? _____

6. Write a sentence that gives the weight of the riders. _____

   _____

▬ Look Back ▬

7. Compare the weight you found in Item 5 to
   your estimate in Item 4. How can you use
   these two answers to see if your answer is correct? _____

   _____

   _____

   _____

8. Show another way to check your answer. _____

SOLVE ANOTHER PROBLEM

A dog weighs 84.8 kg. Carrying a backpack
filled with some cans of food, the dog weighs
about 100 kg. What is the weight of the cans of food? _____

Kristin wants to put organic garbage in a compost pile. She staked out a triangular area on the ground that has two sides of 6 and 8 feet. If the perimeter of the pile is 21 feet, how long is the third side?

━ Understand ━

1. What are you asked to find? _____

2. What are the lengths of two of the sides? _____

3. What is the perimeter? _____

4. How do you find the perimeter of a triangle? _____

━ Plan ━

5. Write an addition equation to help you solve the problem. Let s = the length of the side you do not know. _____

6. Which of the following is a reasonable range for the length of the third side? _____

    a. Less than 5 feet   **b.** Between 5 and 10 feet   **c.** More than 10 feet

━ Solve ━

7. Solve the equation. What is the length of the unknown side? _____

8. Write a sentence describing the size and shape of the compost pile. _____

_____

_____

━ Look Back ━

9. Write a subtraction equation that you could use to find the length of the third side. _____

SOLVE ANOTHER PROBLEM

Kristin staked out a rectangular area on the ground that has one side measuring 6 feet. If the perimeter of the pile is 28 feet, how long are the other sides?

_____

Robert and his granddaughter Bailey built a playhouse. The foundation
of the playhouse was a 1.86 m-by-95 cm rectangle. What was the
perimeter of Bailey's playhouse? Explain.

▬ Understand ▬

1. What are you asked to find? _____

2. What size and shape is the foundation? _____

3. How would you find the perimeter of the foundation?

_____

_____

▬ Plan ▬

4. Both dimensions should be in the same unit.
What will you do to convert meters to centimeters? _____

5. How many centimeters equal 1.86 meters? _____

▬ Solve ▬

6. Find the perimeter of the foundation in centimeters. _____

7. Explain. How did you find your answer? _____

_____

_____

▬ Look Back ▬

8. What is another way you could find the perimeter of the playhouse? _____

_____

_____

SOLVE ANOTHER PROBLEM

Allan and Yolanda built a bookcase. The base of the bookcase was a
1.5 m-by-62 cm rectangle. What was the perimeter of their bookcase?
Explain.

_____

© Scott Foresman Addison Wesley 6

Name _____

Patti made this drawing to help her remember the conversion factor for quarts and gallons.

a. How many quarts are in a gallon?

b. How many quarts are in 4 gallons?

c. How many gallons are in 32 quarts?

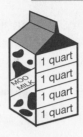

1 gallon

━━ Understand ━━

1. How many conversions are you asked to make? _____

2. What information is given in the drawing? _____

━━ Plan ━━

3. Will you multiply or divide to convert quarts to gallons? _____

4. Will you multiply or divide to convert gallons to quarts? _____

5. By which number will you multiply or divide by? _____

━━ Solve ━━

6. Use your answers to Items 3, 4, and 5.

   a. How many quarts are in a gallon? _____

   b. How many quarts are in 4 gallons? _____

   c. How many gallons are in 32 quarts? _____

━━ Look Back ━━

7. How could you have found the answer with a different method? _____

_____

SOLVE ANOTHER PROBLEM

Curtis made this drawing to help him remember the conversion factor for ounces and pounds.

a. How many ounces are in a pound? _____

b. How many ounces are in 8 pounds? _____

c. How many pounds are in 176 ounces? _____

1 ounce	1 ounce
1 ounce	1 ounce
1 ounce	1 ounce
1 ounce	1 ounce
1 ounce	1 ounce
1 ounce	1 ounce
1 ounce	1 ounce
1 ounce	1 ounce

1 pound

Name _____

The perimeter of a rectangular bookstore is 220 ft, and its length is 50 ft. What is the annual rent for the bookstore if the rent is $20 per square foot each year? Explain.

▬ Understand ▬

1. Circle the perimeter, length, and annual rent of the bookstore.

2. The rent is per square foot. How do you find the number of square feet in a rectangular figure? _____

▬ Plan ▬

3. You are given the length of one side of the bookstore. What is the length of the opposite side of the bookstore? _____

4. Given the perimeter, how can you use the length of two opposite sides to find the width of the other two sides in a rectangle? _____

_____

5. What is the width of the bookstore? _____

6. What operation will you use to find the annual rent? _____

▬ Solve ▬

7. Write a number sentence to find the number of square feet. _____

8. Find the annual rent for the bookstore. _____

9. Explain why it was necessary to follow the steps above. _____

_____

▬ Look Back ▬

10. Explain how drawing a diagram could help you solve this problem.

_____

_____

SOLVE ANOTHER PROBLEM

The perimeter of a rectangular bookstore is 180 ft, and its length is 50 ft. What is the annual rent for the bookstore if the rent is $25 per square foot each year? Explain.

_____

Jaspar drew a parallelogram with a base of 2 cm and a height of 2 cm.
He drew another with base 2 cm and height 4 cm and a third with base
2 cm and height 8 cm. If Jaspar continues drawing parallelograms in this
pattern, what will the area of the sixth shape be?

━━ Understand ━━

1. Circle the information you need.

2. You are to find the area of the parallelogram in the _____ place in the
pattern.

3. What is the formula for
finding the area of a parallelogram? _____

━━ Plan ━━

4. Draw a picture of the three shapes in the pattern.
Label each base and height.

5. What pattern do you see? _____

_____

━━ Solve ━━

6. What are the measures of the base
and height of the sixth parallelogram? _____

7. What is the area of the sixth parallelogram? _____

━━ Look Back ━━

8. What other strategy could you use to find the pattern? _____

_____

SOLVE ANOTHER PROBLEM

Toi drew a parallelogram with a base of 3 cm and a height of
2 cm. She drew another with base 4 cm and height 3 cm and a
third with base 5 cm and height 4 cm. If Toi continues drawing
parallelograms in this pattern, what will the area of the seventh shape be? _____

Name _____

The Bermuda Triangle is a region in the Atlantic Ocean where ships and airplanes are reported to have mysteriously disappeared since the 1940's. Use the diagram to find the area of the Bermuda Triangle.

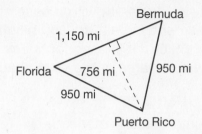

▬ Understand ▬▬

1. What are you asked to find? _____

2. Circle the information in the picture which will help you solve the problem.

▬ Plan ▬▬▬▬

3. What is the formula for finding the area of a triangle? _____

4. **a.** What is the base of the Bermuda Triangle? _____

   b. What is the height of the Bermuda Triangle? _____

5. Which of the following is a reasonable answer? _____

   a. About 200,000 mi^2 **b.** About 400,000 mi^2 **c.** About 800,000 mi^2

▬ Solve ▬▬▬▬

6. Substitute the values for base and height in the formula.

   _____ × _____ ÷ _____ = _____

7. Write a sentence stating the area of the Bermuda Triangle. _____
   _____

▬ Look Back ▬▬

8. Why did you write your answer in square miles? _____
   _____

SOLVE ANOTHER PROBLEM

Find the area of the triangle.

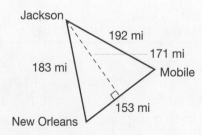

_____

Name _____

Pat's bicycle has a wheel of radius 13 inches. If she rides the bicycle 1 mile (63,360 inches), how many times has the wheel rotated? Explain.

━━ Understand ━━

1. What are you asked to find? _____

2. The _____ of the bicycle wheel is the same as one rotation of the wheel.

3. What is the value of pi? _____

4. Circle the information you need.

━━ Plan ━━

5. What is the diameter of the wheel? _____

6. What is the circumference of the wheel? _____

7. Write an expression for the number of rotations. _____

━━ Solve ━━

8. How many times does the wheel rotate? _____

9. Explain how you can find the answer. _____

_____

_____

━━ Look Back ━━

10. How could you find the number of rotations only using division? _____

_____

| SOLVE ANOTHER PROBLEM |

If the radius of Pat's bicycle wheel were 15 inches and she rode her bicycle for 2 miles, how many times would the wheel rotate? Explain.

_____

_____

A sand dollar is an animal that lives slightly buried in the sand of shallow coastal waters. Its thin, circular body is about 2 to 4 inches wide. What are the smallest and largest areas of sand dollars?

▬ Understand ▬

1. Which mathematical term describes the "width" of a circle? _____

2. You need to find the area of how many sand dollars? _____

▬ Plan ▬

3. What is the formula for finding the area of a circle? _____

4. To convert diameter to radius, you divide the diameter by _____.

5. What is the value of pi to the nearest hundredth? _____

▬ Solve ▬

6. What is the radius of the smallest sand dollar? _____

   Substitute the values of the radius and pi in the formula for finding area of a circle.

   _____ × _____ = _____

7. What is the area of the smallest sand dollar? _____

8. What is the radius of the largest sand dollar? _____

   Substitute the values of the radius and pi in the formula for finding area of a circle.

   _____ × _____ = _____

9. What is the area of the largest sand dollar? _____

▬ Look Back ▬

10. How could you estimate to see if your answer is reasonable? _____

_____

| SOLVE ANOTHER PROBLEM |

What is the area of a sand dollar that has a circular body that is 3 inches wide? _____

Name _____

Sheetal is painting a cardboard cutout for her school's annual haunted house. The cardboard is a triangle 7 feet tall and 7 feet wide. It has a square opening as shown. How many square feet does Sheetal need to paint? Explain your reasoning.

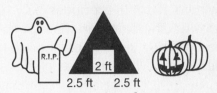

2.5 ft   2 ft   2.5 ft

━━ Understand ━━

1. What are you asked to find? _____

2. Underline the measurements of the triangle's height and width.

━━ Plan ━━

3. What is the formula for the area of the triangle? _____

4. What is the formula for the area of the square? _____

5. Will you add or subtract to find the area to be painted? _____

━━ Solve ━━

6. What is the area of the triangle? _____ Of the square? _____

7. Write a number sentence to show how to find the painted area.

_____

8. How many square feet will Sheetal paint? Explain. _____

_____

━━ Look Back ━━

9. Draw an example of what the cardboard might look like if Sheetal needed to paint the combined areas of the square and the triangle.

_____

SOLVE ANOTHER PROBLEM

Liam is painting a cardboard cutout. The cardboard is a square with 8-ft sides, and it has a circular opening as shown. About how many square feet does Liam need to paint? Explain your reasoning.

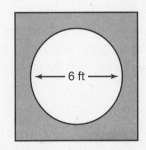

← 6 ft →

_____

Name _____

Marvel Models produces 53,716 model cars each month. They want to
design shipping cartons that hold more than 3 but fewer than 10 models
each. They want to pack each month's cars in their cartons, with no cars
left over. What are their choices? Explain.

━━ Understand ━━

1. Underline what you are asked to find.

2. Circle the information you need.

━━ Plan ━━

3. To find which carton sizes to use for shipping, use divisibility
   rules or division to test 53,716 for divisibility by 4, 5, 6, 7, 8, and 9.
   If 53,716 is evenly divisible by the carton size, then all the models
   can be shipped using that sized carton.

   Is 53,716 evenly divisible

   a. by 4? _____   **b.** by 5? _____   **c.** by 6? _____

   d. by 7? _____   **e.** by 8? _____   **f.** by 9? _____

━━ Solve ━━

4. Which number is 53,716 evenly divisible by? _____

5. Write a sentence to tell which size cartons can be used by Marvel Models.

   _____

━━ Look Back ━━

6. How do you know that you checked all the possible carton sizes
   given in the problem?

   _____

   _____

| SOLVE ANOTHER PROBLEM |

The Pool Company is shipping 5325 wading pools. They want to
design shipping cartons that hold 2, 3, 5, 6, 9, or 10 pools each. They
want to pack each month's pools in their cartons with no pools left
over. What are their choices? Explain.

_____

_____

© Scott Foresman Addison Wesley 6

Mr. Armond has 36 students in his math class. He wants to put them into groups of the same size. He also wants the number in each group to be a prime factor of 36. What are his choices?

Understand

1. What are you asked to find?

_____

_____

Plan

2. To find the possible group sizes, find the prime factors of 36.

Complete the factor tree to find the prime factors.

36 = _____ × _____ × _____ × _____

Solve

3. Which numbers are the prime factors of 36? _____

4. Write a sentence to tell how many students could be in each group.

_____

Look Back

5. How could you have found the answer using another method?

_____

_____

SOLVE ANOTHER PROBLEM

Cassie is lining up 45 students in the pep squad. She wants each row to have the same number of students. She also wants the number of students in each row to be a prime number. What are her options?

_____

In a middle school, the principal plans to hide prizes in the new lockers for the students. The principal plans to put a binder in every 10th locker, a school tee shirt in every in every 15th locker, and a new backpack in every 50th locker. If she starts counting at locker number 1, what is the number of the first locker in which the principal will put all three prizes?

━━ Understand ━━

1. Restate the problem in your own words.

_____

_____

_____

2. Underline the information you need.

━━ Plan ━━

3. Find the least common multiple for 10, 15, and 50.

   a. List multiples of 10:

   _____

   b. List multiples of 15: _____

   c. List multiples of 50: _____

━━ Solve ━━

4. What is the least common multiple of 10, 15, and 50? _____

5. Which will be the first locker to contain a binder, a tee shirt, and

   a backpack? _____

━━ Look Back ━━

6. What is another way you could solve the problem?

_____

SOLVE ANOTHER PROBLEM

Ernesto, Michelina, and Kale volunteer at the zoo. Ernesto works every 5 days. Michelina works every 6 days. Kale works every 15 days. They work together today. How many days will it be until the next time they work together? _____

Name _____

Name two fractions that describe the number of square picture frames. Identify the numerators and denominators.

Understand

1. What are you asked to do?

_____

_____

Plan

2. What will the numerator describe? _____

3. What will the denominator describe? _____

Solve

4. How many picture frames are shaped like squares? _____

5. How many picture frames are there in all? _____

6. What are two fractions that describe the number of square picture frames?

_____

7. What are the numerators in the two fractions you wrote? _____

8. What are the denominators in the two fractions you wrote? _____

Look Back

9. What two other equivalent fractions could you write for the number of square picture frames? _____

SOLVE ANOTHER PROBLEM

Name two fractions that describe the number of shaded rectangles. One of the fractions should have 10 as the denominator. Identify the numerators and denominators.

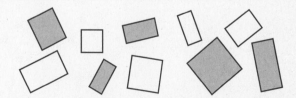

Name _____

Marilyn sold $\frac{3}{6}$ of the raffle tickets at a carnival. Darren sold $\frac{2}{8}$ of them. Jamelya sold the rest. Who sold more tickets, Marilyn by herself, or Darren and Jamelya together? Explain.

━━ Understand ━━

1. Restate the problem in your own words. _____

_____

_____

━━ Plan ━━

2. Which strategy could you use to solve the problem? _____

    a. Make a Table   **b.** Look for a Pattern   **c.** Solve a Simpler Problem

━━ Solve ━━

3. If 6 tickets were sold, how many tickets did Marilyn sell? _____

4. If 6 tickets were sold, how many tickets did Darren and Jamelya sell? _____

5. Compare the number of tickets Marilyn sold to the number of tickets Darren and Jamelya sold. Who sold more tickets? Explain.

_____

_____

_____

━━ Look Back ━━

6. What other strategies could you use to solve the problem?

_____

┌─────────────────────────────────┐
│   **SOLVE ANOTHER PROBLEM**   │
└─────────────────────────────────┘

Casey ate $\frac{3}{8}$ of a pizza. Ann ate $\frac{2}{8}$ of the pizza and Juan ate the rest. Who ate more pizza, Juan by himself, or Casey and Ann together?

_____

Caesar has a tool box that is $15\frac{3}{4}$ in. long. His hammer is $\frac{45}{4}$ in. long. Will the hammer fit in the tool box?

━━ Understand ━━

1. What do you need to find?

_____

2. Circle the information you need.

━━ Plan ━━

3. For the hammer to fit in the tool box, should the length of the hammer be longer or shorter than the length of the tool box? _____

4. Write $\frac{45}{4}$ as a mixed number. _____

5. Compare the whole number of the number you wrote in Item 4 with the whole number in $15\frac{3}{4}$. Which is greater? _____

━━ Solve ━━

6. Will the hammer fit in the tool box? Explain how you know.

_____

_____

_____

━━ Look Back ━━

7. Can you think of another way to solve the problem? Explain.

_____

_____

SOLVE ANOTHER PROBLEM

Yoko has $2\frac{5}{8}$ pounds of trail mix in one bag. Sam has $\frac{10}{8}$ pounds of trail mix in ten bags. Who has more trail mix? Explain how you know.

_____

_____

Melissa is using a set of wrenches that come in these sizes:
0.125 inch, 0.25 inch, 0.375 inch, 0.5 inch, 0.625 inch, 0.75 inch,
and 0.875 inch. Write each wrench size as a fraction in lowest terms.

━━ Understand ━━

1. What are you asked to find?

_____

━━ Plan ━━

2. Write the steps to follow when you write a decimal as a fraction.

_____

_____

3. Use your rule to write 0.125 as a fraction. _____

4. Find the greatest common factor for the numerator and denominator. _____

━━ Solve ━━

5. Use the greatest common factor to write the fraction in lowest terms. _____

6. Repeat steps 3 through 5 for the remaining decimals.

    a. 0.25 _____   **b.** 0.375 _____   **c.** 0.5 _____

    d. 0.625 _____   **e.** 0.75 _____   **f.** 0.875 _____

━━ Look Back ━━

7. Check your answers by converting the fractions to decimals.
Are the decimals you find the same as the original decimals?

_____

_____

SOLVE ANOTHER PROBLEM

Timothy bought some salads for a party. The salads weighed
0.6 pound, 0.25 pound, 0.15 pound, and 0.375 pound. Write each
weight as a fraction in lowest terms.

_____

$\frac{3}{5}$ of the tourists who visit Florida come during the summer. $\frac{3}{10}$ travel to Florida during the winter. During which season does Florida get more tourists?

━━ Understand ━━

1. Underline the question.

2. What fraction of tourists visit Florida in the summer? _____

3. What fraction of tourists visit Florida in the winter? _____

━━ Plan ━━

4. Find a common denominator for $\frac{3}{5}$ and $\frac{3}{10}$. _____

5 Rewrite each fraction using the common denominator. _____

━━ Solve ━━

6. Compare the fractions. Which fraction is greater? _____

7. When do more tourists visit Florida—summer or winter? _____

━━ Look Back ━━

8. How could you have solved the problem in a different way?

_____

_____

9. Use your answer to the problem to make a generalization. If two fractions have the same numerator, which is the greater fraction?

_____

SOLVE ANOTHER PROBLEM

Manny, Anita, and Taylor shared the driving on a trip. Manny drove $\frac{1}{8}$ of the distance. Anita drove $\frac{1}{4}$ of the distance. Did Manny or Anita drive more miles? Explain how you know.

_____

Sandra makes bracelets, necklaces, and chokers using leather string.
A bracelet requires $\frac{7}{12}$ ft of string, and a necklace requires $\frac{22}{12}$ ft. She
has $\frac{81}{12}$ ft, which is exactly enough to make 3 bracelets, 2 necklaces,
and 1 choker. How much string does each choker require? Explain.

■ Understand ■

1. Circle what you are asked to find.

2. How much leather string does Sandra have? _____

3. Underline the amount of string needed to make a bracelet and
   a necklace.

■ Plan ■

4. Which operation will you use to find the amount of string needed to make

   3 bracelets? _____   2 necklaces? _____

5. Which operation will you use to find the string
   left over after making the bracelets and necklaces? _____

■ Solve ■

6. Write a number sentence showing the
   amount of string needed to make 3 bracelets. _____

7. How much string is needed to make 2 necklaces? _____

8. How much string is needed to make 3 bracelets and 2 necklaces? _____

9. How much string will Sandra have left to make one choker? Explain. _____

   _____

   _____

■ Look Back ■

10. What other operation could you have used to
    find the amount of string needed to make 3 bracelets? _____

┌─────────────────────────────────┐
│   **SOLVE ANOTHER PROBLEM**   │
└─────────────────────────────────┘

Sandra also makes belts. She has $\frac{92}{12}$ feet of string,
which is enough to make 2 bracelets, 2 necklaces, and
1 belt. A bracelet requires $\frac{7}{12}$ feet and a necklace requires
$\frac{22}{12}$ feet of string. How much string does each belt require? _____

Name _____

A recipe for fruit punch calls for $\frac{3}{8}$ of a quart of lemon drink, $\frac{3}{2}$ of a quart of orange juice, $\frac{1}{10}$ of a quart of cranberry juice, and $\frac{3}{4}$ of a quart of soda water. How large a container is needed for the punch? Explain.

Understand

1. Underline the quantity for each ingredient in the punch.

Plan

2. What is the least common denominator for the ingredients? _____

3. Write an equivalent fraction using the least common denominator.

   a. $\frac{3}{8}$ _____   **b.** $\frac{3}{2}$ _____   **c.** $\frac{1}{10}$ _____   **d.** $\frac{3}{4}$ _____

4. Which operation will you use to find the total quantity of punch? _____

5. Which of the following is a reasonable answer? _____

   a. less than 1 qt   **b.** about 1 qt   **c.** more than 1 qt

Solve

6. How much punch does the recipe make? _____

7. Think about how much liquid most pitchers and punch bowls hold. What is a reasonable size container for the punch? Explain. _____

_____

_____

Look Back

8. What should you do if the size container you chose in Item 7 does *not* fall within the range you chose for Item 5? _____

_____

SOLVE ANOTHER PROBLEM

A recipe for party mix calls for $\frac{3}{4}$ of a cup of cereal, $\frac{1}{4}$ of a cup of peanuts, $\frac{5}{8}$ of a cup of pretzels, and $\frac{1}{2}$ of a cup of crackers. How many cups are in the mix? How large a container is needed? Explain. _____

_____

_____

The perimeter of the lid to Janice's rectangular jewelry box is $\frac{10}{4}$ of a yard. If the longer sides are $\frac{3}{4}$ of a yard, how long are the shorter sides? Explain.

Understand

1. Circle the perimeter and underline the length of one side of the lid.

2. How do you find the perimeter? _____

Plan

3. Draw a picture of the jewelry box.
   Label the longer sides.

4. Write an equation to find the length of the two longer sides. _____

5. Use your answer to Item 4 to write an equation showing the length of the two shorter sides. _____

Solve

6. The sum of two fractions equals your answer to Item 5. The denominator of each of the two fractions will be _____.

   Use Guess and Check to find each numerator. Each numerator is _____.

7. What is the length of each shorter side? _____

8. Explain _____

   _____

Look Back

9. What is a different way to find the answer? _____

   _____

SOLVE ANOTHER PROBLEM

The perimeter of the lid to a rectangular box is $\frac{14}{6}$ of a yard. If the longer sides are $\frac{5}{6}$ of a yard, how long are the shorter sides? Explain. _____

_____

© Scott Foresman Addison Wesley 6

Dimitri lives near the Colorado River. He should evacuate his
home when the river reaches 28 feet. The river is now at $21\frac{7}{10}$ feet
and is predicted to rise another $6\frac{1}{2}$ feet this evening. Will Dimitri
need to evacuate?

━━ Understand ━━

1. Dimitri should evacuate when the river reaches what level? _____

2. What is the level of the river now? _____

3. How much is the river predicted to rise this evening? _____

━━ Plan ━━

4. Will you use addition or subtraction to decide
whether or not Dimitri will need to evacuate? _____

5. To round a mixed number, should you drop the
fraction if it is more than $\frac{1}{2}$ or if it is less than $\frac{1}{2}$? _____

━━ Solve ━━

6. Round the mixed numbers. Write an equation to tell
how high the river will be if it rises as much as predicted. _____

7. Will the river reach 28 feet? _____

8. Write a sentence to tell whether or not Dimitri will need to evacuate. _____

_____

_____

━━ Look Back ━━

9. Could you draw a picture to help you find the answer? Explain. _____

_____

_____

© Scott Foresman Addison Wesley 6

┌─────────────────────────────────┐
│   **SOLVE ANOTHER PROBLEM**   │
└─────────────────────────────────┘

Suppose Dimitri will need to evacuate when the river
reaches 30 feet. The river is predicted to rise $5\frac{7}{12}$ feet
from its present level of $21\frac{7}{10}$ feet. Will he need to evacuate? _____

The combined area of Shapes A and B is $4\frac{2}{3}$ m^2. The area of Shape B is $1\frac{1}{3}$ m^2 more than the area of Shape A. Find the areas of both shapes.

━━ Understand ━━

1. What are you asked to find? _____

2. What is the combined area of the shapes? _____

3. How much larger is Shape B than Shape A? _____

━━ Plan ━━

The diagram represents the combined area of the two shapes. Use the diagram to answer the questions.

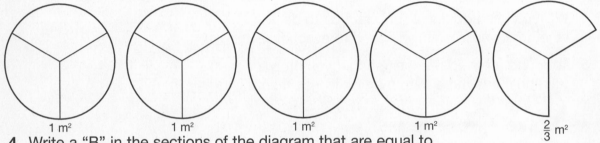

1 m^2 1 m^2 1 m^2 1 m^2 $\frac{2}{3}$ m^2

4. Write a "B" in the sections of the diagram that are equal to difference in the areas of Shape B and Shape A.

5. With the difference accounted for, the area of Shape A equals the area of Shape B. Write an "A" for Shape A and a "B" for Shape B in the remaining sections.

━━ Solve ━━

6. Use the sections labeled "A" in the diagram to write the area of Shape A. _____

7. Use the sections labeled "B" in the diagram to write the area of Shape B. _____

━━ Look Back ━━

8. Write and solve an addition equation to check your answer.

_____

SOLVE ANOTHER PROBLEM

The combined area of Shapes C and D is $8\frac{3}{4}$ in^2. The area of Shape D is $2\frac{1}{4}$ in^2 more than the area of Shape C. Find the areas of both shapes.

_____

Name _____

A large financial institution trading on the New York Stock Exchange listed its highest selling price in the last year at $80\frac{3}{8}$ points. The difference between its highest and lowest prices was $26\frac{1}{2}$ points. Write and solve an equation to find the lowest selling price.

━━ Understand ━━

1. What is the highest selling price of the stock? _____

2. What is the difference between its highest and lowest prices? _____

━━ Plan ━━

3. What is the least common denominator for $\frac{3}{8}$ and $\frac{1}{2}$? _____

4. Write the prices using the least common denominator.

    a. Highest selling price _____   **b.** Difference in selling price _____

5. Which operation will you use to find the difference? _____

6. When you write the equation, which variable will you use to represent the value of the lowest selling price of the stock? _____

━━ Solve ━━

7. Write an equation to find the lowest selling price. _____

8. Solve the equation. What is the lowest selling price? _____

━━ Look Back ━━

9. Write an equation that will find the lowest selling price using another operation.

_____

SOLVE ANOTHER PROBLEM

The highest selling price of the stock was $75\frac{3}{4}$. The difference between its highest and lowest prices was $18\frac{1}{8}$. Write and solve an equation to find the lowest selling price.

_____

Give five pairs of values for x and y so that $5\frac{x}{y}$ will round to 6 when rounded to the nearest whole number. What do all of your pairs of numbers have in common?

━━ Understand ━━

1. Which whole number are you asked to round $5\frac{x}{y}$ to? _____

━━ Plan ━━

2. Will you round $5\frac{x}{y}$ up or down? _____

3. If a fraction is less than $\frac{1}{2}$ will you round
up or down to the nearest whole number? _____

4. Will the fractional part of $5\frac{x}{y}$ be
less than or greater than or equal to $\frac{1}{2}$? _____

━━ Solve ━━

5. Complete the table. Give five pairs
of values for x and y so that $5\frac{x}{y}$ will
round to 6.

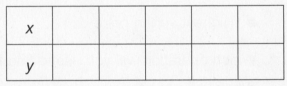

x					
y					

6. What do all the pairs of numbers have in common?

_____

_____

━━ Look Back ━━

7. Why did you decide whether to round $5\frac{x}{y}$ up
or down before deciding on values for x and y? _____

_____

_____

SOLVE ANOTHER PROBLEM

Complete the table. Give five pairs of
values for x and y so that $5\frac{x}{y}$ will round
to 5 when rounded to the nearest whole
number. What do all of your pairs of
numbers have in common?

x					
y					

_____

_____

Name _____

Castile soap is named for the kingdom of Castile in Spain where the soap was first produced. To make about 36 bars, 1 pound 9 ounces of olive oil is needed. If a pound of olive oil costs $8.00, how much does the olive oil for this recipe cost? Explain.

━━ Understand ━━

1. Underline what you are asked to find.

2. What is the cost per pound of the olive oil? _____

3. How much olive oil is used to make 36 bars of soap? _____

━━ Plan ━━

4. There are 16 ounces in one pound. How many ounces of olive oil are used to make 36 bars of soap? _____

5. Write the quantity of olive oil as an improper fraction. _____

6. Write an expression to show how to find the cost of the olive oil used in 36 bars of Castile soap. _____

━━ Solve ━━

7. What is the cost to make 36 bars of soap?. _____

8. Explain how you found the answer. _____

_____

_____

━━ Look Back ━━

9. How could you find your answer in a different way? _____

_____

_____

SOLVE ANOTHER PROBLEM

To make about 72 bars, 3 pounds 2 ounces of olive oil is needed. If a pound of olive oil costs $9.00, how much does the olive oil for this recipe cost? Round your answer to the nearest cent. Explain.

_____

To make $\frac{3}{4}$ cup of powdered-milk paint, you mix $\frac{1}{2}$ cup of powdered nonfat milk and $\frac{1}{2}$ cup of water. Adjust this recipe to make one whole cup of paint. Explain your method.

━━ Understand ━━

1. Circle the quantity of paint that is made from the recipe.

2. Underline the quantities of the paint ingredients.

━━ Plan ━━

3. How many fourths are in $\frac{3}{4}$? _____

4. To rewrite the recipe for $\frac{1}{4}$ cup of paint, you could divide each quantity by the number in Item 3 or multiply by _____.

5. Once the recipe has been written for $\frac{1}{4}$ cup of paint, you can rewrite it for 1 cup of paint by multiplying each quantity by _____.

━━ Solve ━━

6. Complete the table for $\frac{1}{4}$ cup of paint. Then use your answer to find the quantities for 1 cup of paint.

Paint (cups)	Milk (cups)	Water (cups)
$\frac{3}{4}$	$\frac{1}{2}$	$\frac{1}{2}$
$\frac{1}{4}$		
1		

7. Explain how you found the quantities.

_____

_____

━━ Look Back ━━

8. Explain how you could use division to rewrite the recipe. _____

_____

SOLVE ANOTHER PROBLEM

To make $\frac{3}{4}$ cup of powdered-milk paint, you mix $\frac{1}{2}$ cup of powdered nonfat milk and $\frac{1}{2}$ cup of water. Adjust this recipe to make $1\frac{1}{8}$ cup of paint. Explain your method. _____

Name _____

As a result of the 1990 census, Pennsylvania has 21 seats in the House of Representatives. This is $\frac{7}{10}$ as many seats as Texas has. How many seats does Texas have?

━ Understand ━

1. Underline what you are asked to find.

2. How many seats did Pennsylvania have as a result of the 1990 census? _____

3. The number of Representatives from Pennsylvania is what fraction of the number of Representatives from Texas? _____

━ Plan ━

4. Will Texas have fewer or more Representatives than Pennsylvania? _____

5. Which operation will you use to find the number of seats Texas has in the House of Representatives? _____

6. Which would be a reasonable number of seats for Texas to have in the House of Representatives? _____

   a. 15 seats   b. 21 seats   c. 30 seats

━ Solve ━

7. Write an equation showing the number of seats Texas has in the House of Representatives. _____

8. How many seats does Texas have? _____

━ Look Back ━

9. How could you use decimals to find your answer? _____

_____

_____

| SOLVE ANOTHER PROBLEM |

As a result of the 1990 census, Colorado has 6 seats in the House of Representatives. This is $\frac{3}{10}$ as many seats as Illinois has. How many seats does Illinois have? _____

Name _____

The size of letters in printed material such as newspapers or books is measured in points. One point equals $\frac{1}{72}$ of an inch.

a. What is the point size of type that is $\frac{1}{8}$ of an inch high?

b. What is the point size of type that is $1\frac{1}{2}$ inches high?

━━ Understand ━━

1. What part of an inch is equal to one point? _____

2. What are you asked to find? _____

_____

━━ Plan ━━

3. Will each type size be more than or less than 72 points?

   a. $\frac{1}{8}$ inch type _____

   b. $1\frac{1}{2}$ inches _____

4. Write $1\frac{1}{2}$ as an improper fraction. _____

5. Write an expression to show how to use division to find each point size.

   a. $\frac{1}{8}$ inch type _____

   b. $1\frac{1}{2}$ inches _____

━━ Solve ━━

6. Simplify your expressions to find the number of points in each.

   a. $\frac{1}{8}$ inch type _____   **b.** $1\frac{1}{2}$ inches _____

━━ Look Back ━━

7. How can you use multiplication to check your answer? _____

_____

SOLVE ANOTHER PROBLEM

What is the point size of type that is $\frac{1}{6}$ of an inch? _____

Length was once measured in palms and spans. One inch equaled $\frac{1}{3}$ of a palm and $\frac{1}{9}$ of a span.

a. Which equation could you use to find the number of palms in 12 inches?

    A $p \div \frac{1}{3} = 12$ **B** $\frac{1}{3}p = 12$

b. How many palms are in 12 inches?

c. Write and solve an equation to find the number of spans in 18 inches.

▬ Understand ▬

1. How many palms equal one inch? _____ How many spans? _____

▬ Plan ▬

2. In division, you break down a given amount into equal parts. In multiplication, you find how many items in all. Which operation will you use to find how many

    a. palms are in 12 inches?   **b.** spans are in 18 inches?

    _____   _____

3. How are the equations used to find the number of palms in 12 inches and the number of spans in 18 inches similar? _____

_____

▬ Solve ▬

4. Which equation would you use to find the number of palms? _____

5. How many palms are in 12 inches? _____

6. Write an equation to find the number of spans in 18 inches. _____

7. How many spans are in 18 inches? _____

▬ Look Back ▬

8. How can you check your answer? _____

_____

SOLVE ANOTHER PROBLEM

Write and solve an equation to find the number of inches in 16 palms.

_____

Choose the lines that are parallel.

(A) *A* and *D*   (B) *C* and *E*

(C) *A* and *C*   (D) *E* and *D*

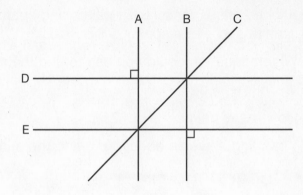

Understand

1. What are you asked to do? _____

2. Do parallel lines intersect? _____

Plan

3. Circle all pairs of parallel lines in the diagram.

4. How many pairs of parallel lines did you circle? _____

Solve

5. Write the letters of all the pairs of parallel lines. _____

6. Compare your answer to Item 5 with the given answer choices.

   a Choice (A) says lines A and D are parallel. Is that correct? _____

   b. Choice (B) says lines C and E are parallel. Is that correct? _____

   c. Choice (C) says lines A and C are parallel. Is that correct? _____

   d. Choice (D) says lines E and D are parallel. Is that correct? _____

7. Which choice—A, B, C, or D—is the correct answer? _____

Look Back

8. Why are lines A and B not the correct answer? _____

_____

| SOLVE ANOTHER PROBLEM |

Which lines in the diagram above are perpendicular?

_____

Name _____

Tell whether this statement is always, sometimes, or never true.

Two acute angles of the same size form a right angle.

━━ Understand ━━

1. What part of an index card forms a right angle? _____

2. Is an acute angle smaller or greater than a right angle? _____

3. How many acute angles are you asked to find? _____

4. Are the acute angles the same or different sizes? _____

━━ Plan ━━

5. Draw a right angle. Then draw a line to divide the right triangle into two angles of the same size.

6. Are the two angles in Item 5 acute angles? _____

7. Draw two acute angles of different sizes. Then use one side of each angle to draw another angle the same size.

First angle   Second angle

8. Do both pairs of acute angles you drew in Item 7 form right angles? Explain. _____

_____

━━ Solve ━━

9. Use your answers to Items 6 and 8 to tell whether the statement is always, sometimes, or never true. _____

━━ Look Back ━━

10. What other strategy could you use to find the answer?

_____

| SOLVE ANOTHER PROBLEM |

Is the statement always, sometimes, or never true:
"Three acute angles of the same size form a straight angle." _____

Name _____

Estimate the measurement of the
obtuse angle.

(A) 45°   (B) 135°

(C) 90°   (D) 270°za

━━ Understand ━━━

1. What is the definition of an obtuse angle? _____

_____

2. Which of these kinds of angles are shown in the diagram? _____

    a. acute and right   **b.** right and obtuse   **c.** acute and obtuse

━━ Plan ━━━━

3. Darken the rays that make up the obtuse angle in the diagram.

4. Classify the type of angle given in each choice as acute, obtuse,
right, or none of these.

    a. Choice A (45°) _____   **b.** Choice B (135°) _____

    c. Choice C (90°) _____   **d.** Choice D (270°) _____

━━ Solve ━━━

5. Which choice is an obtuse angle? _____

━━ Look Back ━━━

6. Why does classifying the angle help estimate the measure?

_____

_____

SOLVE ANOTHER PROBLEM

Which of the answer choices is a reasonable estimate for
the measurement of the acute angle in the drawing above? _____

(A) 45°   (B) 135°

(C) 90°   (D) 270°

A triangle has angles *A, B,* and *C.* The complement of ∠A is 58° and the supplement of ∠B is 60°. What is the measure of ∠C? Explain your strategy.

▬ Understand ▬

1. Which angle's measurement are you to find? _____

2. Underline the information you need.

▬ Plan ▬

3. What is sum of the measures of two complementary angles? _____

4. The complement of ∠A is 58°. What is the measure of ∠A? _____

5. What is sum of the measures of two supplementary angles? _____

6. The supplement of ∠B is 60°. What is the measure of ∠B? _____

7. What is sum of the measures of the three angles in a triangle? _____

▬ Solve ▬

8. Add the measurements of ∠A and ∠B: _____ + _____ = _____

9. Find the measure of ∠C: _____ − _____ = _____

10. What is the measure of ∠C? _____

11. What strategy did you use to find the measure of ∠C?

_____

▬ Look Back ▬

12. What other strategies could you use to find the measure of ∠C?

_____

_____

SOLVE ANOTHER PROBLEM

A triangle has angles *D, E,* and *F.* The complement of ∠D is 42° and the supplement of ∠E is 54°. What is the measure of ∠F? _____

Jeremy has two poles for the end of his tent. They are each 4 feet long. Can he form the triangular end of his tent if he puts two pole ends together and places the other ends 9 feet apart?

━━ Understand ━━

1. What figure will be formed by the two poles and the ground? _____

2. What are the lengths of each of the two poles? _____

3. How far apart will Jeremy place the ends of the poles? _____

━━ Plan ━━

4. Is the sum of the two shorter sides of a triangle greater or less than the length of the longer side? _____

5. What is the length of the longest side of the figure formed? _____

6. Write an equation to find the sum of the two shorter tent poles? _____

━━ Solve ━━

7. Is the sum in Item 6 greater than or less than the length of the longest side? _____

8. Can Jeremy place the poles 9 feet apart? _____

━━ Look Back ━━

9. What other strategy could you use to find the answer?

_____

SOLVE ANOTHER PROBLEM

Diana has two poles for the end of her tent. They are each 8 feet long. Can she form the triangular end of her tent if she puts two pole ends together and places the other ends 10 feet apart? Explain.

_____

_____

_____

Name _____

The lengths of the sides of a quadrilateral are 3.5 ft, $\frac{7}{2}$ ft, $3\frac{1}{2}$ ft, and $2\frac{3}{2}$ ft. Is the quadrilateral regular or irregular? Explain.

━ Understand ━

1. Underline the lengths of the sides of the quadrilateral.

2. Circle what the problem asks you to find.

3. How do you know if a polygon is regular? _____

_____

━ Plan ━

4. Write each measure as an improper fraction.

   a. 3.5 _____   **b.** $\frac{7}{2}$ _____   **c.** $3\frac{1}{2}$ _____   **d.** $2\frac{3}{2}$ _____

5. Draw a quadrilateral using the given sides and making sure all 4 angles have the same measure. If possible, draw the quadrilateral using the given sides and making sure that all 4 angles do *not* have the same measure.

━ Solve ━

6. Is the quadrilateral regular or irregular? Explain. _____

_____

_____

━ Look Back ━

7. What ways could you have written the measures other than as improper fractions?

_____

_____

SOLVE ANOTHER PROBLEM

If a pentagon has sides of 2.25 in., $1\frac{5}{4}$ in., $\frac{7}{4}$ in., $2\frac{1}{4}$ in., and 1.75 in., is it regular or irregular? Explain.

_____

Explain why the shape of the
kite shown cannot be classified
as a trapezoid, a parallelogram,
a rhombus, a rectangle, or
a square.

▬ Understand ▬

1. Underline the five quadrilaterals that are *not* classifications of the kite.

▬ Plan ▬

2. Which of the five quadrilaterals can be classified as a parallelogram?

_____

3. What do you know about the sides of a parallelogram? _____

_____

4. What do you know about the sides of the fifth figure? _____

5. Does the kite have any parallel sides? _____

6. Does the kite shape have any pairs of
opposite sides that are the same length? _____

▬ Solve ▬

7. Why can a kite not be classified as any of the given quadrilaterals?

_____

_____

▬ Look Back ▬

8. Does your answer to Item 7 rule out each figure named in the problem? _____

SOLVE ANOTHER PROBLEM

Classify the quadrilaterals that make up the
patterns of the kite in as many ways as possible. _____

_____

© Scott Foresman Addison Wesley 6

A triangle has one angle of 40°. The other angles are congruent to each other. What are the measurements of the other two angles? Explain.

━ Understand ━

1. What is the measurement of the given angle? _____

2. What does *congruent* mean? _____

3. Would congruent angles have the same or different measures? _____

━ Plan ━

4. What is the sum of the measures of the three angles of a triangle? _____

5. Which is a reasonable measure for one of the congruent angles? _____

    a. about 360°   **b.** about 180°   **c.** less than 90°

━ Solve ━

6. Subtract to find the measure of the two congruent angles. _____

7. Write an equation to find the measures of the congruent angles.

_____

8. What are the measures of the congruent angles? _____

━ Look Back ━

9. How could drawing a picture of the triangle help you decide if your answer is reasonable? _____

_____

_____

SOLVE ANOTHER PROBLEM

A parallelogram has two pairs of congruent angles. One angle measures 45°. What are the measurements of the other angles? Explain.

_____

_____

What is the least number of degrees of rotation that will land the flower on top of itself?

━━ Understand ━━

1. Are you looking at rotational or line symmetry? _____

2. Do you want to find the greatest or least number of degrees in the rotation? _____

3. Which is a description of the petals? _____

   a. Congruent   **b.** Evenly spaced   **c.** Both a and c   **d.** Neither a nor b

━━ Plan ━━

4. How many times will the figure "land on itself" when it rotates one complete turn? _____

5. Are the degrees in each rotation the same or different? _____

6. How many degrees are in a complete rotation? _____

━━ Solve ━━

7. Complete the equation to find the number of degrees in each rotation.

   _____ ÷ _____ = _____

━━ Look Back ━━

8. Is the degree of rotation greater if the flower is rotated clockwise or counter clockwise?

   _____

SOLVE ANOTHER PROBLEM

What is the least number of degrees of rotation that will land the flower on top of itself?

_____

Name _____

Draw a tessellation that does not use a polygon as the figure tessellated. Explain your tessellation.

━━ Understand ━━

1. What are you asked to draw? _____

2. What shape figure are you *not* to use in your drawing? _____

━━ Plan ━━

3. Can you use all straight line segments in your drawing? Explain. _____

_____

4. Which of the figures below will tessellate? _____

a. 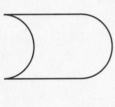   b. 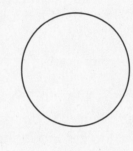   c. 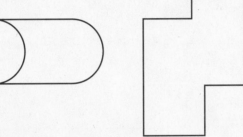   d.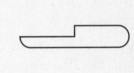

━━ Solve ━━

5. Choose one of the figures in Item 4 that meets the criteria of Item 3. Then make the drawing.

6. Explain. _____

_____

━━ Look Back ━━

7. Draw a different figure to answer the question.

| SOLVE ANOTHER PROBLEM |

Draw a tessellation that does not use a quadrilateral as the figure tessellated. Explain your tessellation.

_____

Order –5, –26, 8, 19, and –20 from least to greatest. Then order these same numbers from closest to zero to furthest from zero. Explain the similarities and differences between your two lists.

━━ Understand ━━

1. Underline the integers you are asked to order.

━━ Plan ━━

2. Show each integer on the number line. Add any necessary labels.

━━ Solve ━━

3. Order the numbers from least to greatest. _____

4. The integer +6 is 6 "steps" from zero. So is the integer –6. How many "steps" is each of the following integers from zero?

    a. –5 _____   **b.** –26 _____   **c.** 8 _____

    d. 19 _____   **e.** –20 _____

5. Use your answers to Item 4 to write the integers in order from closest to zero to furthest from zero. _____

6. How are your lists alike? Different? _____

_____

_____

━━ Look Back ━━

7. How could you write the numbers in order from least to greatest without using a number line? _____

_____

_____

SOLVE ANOTHER PROBLEM

Order 12, –3, 5, –14, 19 from least to greatest. Then order these same numbers from closest to zero to furthest from zero.

_____

Leon had the following test scores to average: 87, 91, 88, 95, and 89. He said, "I guess my average is about 90. My scores are off that by –3, +1, –2, +5, and –1. When I add those numbers, they add to zero. So I must be right." Do you agree with Leon? Explain.

▬ Understand ▬

1. Underline the test scores.

2. Circle the integers that describe how far each test score is from 90.

3. What did Leon state? _____

_____

▬ Plan ▬

4. What is the sum of Leon's test scores? _____

5. How many test scores are listed? _____

▬ Solve ▬

6. Divide the sum of the test scores by the number of tests to find the average (mean) test score. _____

7. Is the average of Leon's test scores 90? Do you agree with Leon? _____

▬ Look Back ▬

8. Why might Leon's method *not* be a useful way to find an average? _____

_____

_____

SOLVE ANOTHER PROBLEM

Ana bowled these scores: 122, 125, 131, and 118. She said, "I guess my average is about 124." Use Leon's method to see if you agree.

_____

_____

Nicki visited her dad at work and got lost in the building. She started
on the first floor. She rode the elevator up 4 floors, then down 2 floors,
then up 6 more floors, then down another floor.

a. Write an expression to represent this situation.

b. If Nicki started on the first floor, which floor did she end up on?

━ Understand ━

1. Underline the sentence that describes the
floors at which Nicki's elevator stopped.

━ Plan ━

2. Draw a diagram of the building. You may
wish to use a vertical number line with
zero representing the ground floor.

3. Will you use a positive or a
negative number to indicate
that Nicki rode the elevator *down*?

_____

4. Write the integer that represents each part of Nicki's elevator ride.

a. Start on the first floor _____   **b.** Up 4 floors _____

c. down 2 floors _____   **d.** Up 6 floors _____   **e.** Down 1 floor _____

━ Solve ━

5. Use the integers in Item 4 to write an expression. _____

6. Simplify your expression to find which floor Nicki ended up on. _____

━ Look Back ━

7. Why was it helpful to draw a diagram? _____

_____

SOLVE ANOTHER PROBLEM

Ty climbed one flight of stairs. He then rode the elevator down 2 floors,
then up 5 floors, then down 3 more floors, then up another floor.

a. Write an expression to represent this situation. _____

b. If Ty started on the ground floor, which floor did he end up on? _____

Name _____

Sal's business currently has expenses of $4 million and sales of $9 million. Sal wants to triple the size of his business. Express the new expenses, sales, and profit as integers.

— Understand —

1. What are the current expenses of Sal's business? _____

2. What are the current sales of Sal's business? _____

3. What does triple mean? _____

— Plan —

4. Tell whether each number will be positive or negative.

   a. Expenses _____   b. Sales _____

5. Which operation will you use to triple each amount? _____

— Solve —

6. What is triple Sal's current expenses? _____

7. What is triple Sal's current sales? _____

8. Profit is the amount remaining after expenses are deducted from sales. Write an equation showing how to find the profit in Sal's business. _____

— Look Back —

9. Could you determine if the profit would be a positive or a negative number without doing any calculations? Explain.

   _____

   _____

SOLVE ANOTHER PROBLEM

Marky's business currently has expenses of $6 million and sales of $8 million. Marky wants to double the size of her business. Express the new expenses, sales, and profit as integers.

_____

_____

Name _____

Use the map and the directions given to find the coordinates of Smallville School.

The school and the marketplace have the same y-coordinate. The x-coordinate of the school is twice the difference between the y-coordinate of the marketplace and the y-coordinate of the gas station.

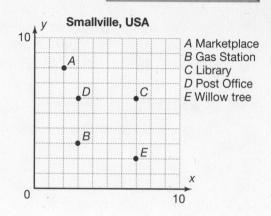

Smallville, USA

A Marketplace
B Gas Station
C Library
D Post Office
E Willow tree

═══ Understand ═══

1. Circle the phrase that tells how to find the y-coordinate of the school.

2. Underline the phrase that tells how to find the x-coordinate of the school.

═══ Plan ═══

3. Which operations will you use to find the x-coordinate of the school? _____

   a. Multiplication, then subtraction   **b.** Subtraction, then multiplication

4. The coordinates of the point for the marketplace are _____

5. The coordinates of the points for gas station are _____

═══ Solve ═══

6. What is the y-coordinate of the ordered pair in Item 4? _____

7. Use the y-coordinates of the ordered pairs you wrote in Items 4 and 5 to write an equation for the x-coordinate of the school. _____

8. What are the coordinates of the school? _____

═══ Look Back ═══

9. Would it have been easier to find the answer by only writing the value of the y-coordinate for each building? Explain. _____

_____

┌─────────────────────────────────┐
│   **SOLVE ANOTHER PROBLEM**   │
└─────────────────────────────────┘

Use the map above and these directions to find the coordinates of the park.

The park and the library have the same x-coordinate. The y-coordinate of the park is one half the sum of the x-coordinate of the post office and the x-coordinate of the library.

_____

One item that Cheryl had to find on a treasure hunt was located at the point (3, 4) on the map. When Cheryl got there, she realized she had the map upside down. How many units left, right, up, and down on the map should Cheryl walk to find the correct location?

━ Understand ━

1. Underline what you are asked to find.

2. Why was Cheryl not at those coordinates? _____

━ Plan ━

3. Mark (3, 4) on the coordinate plane. Label it *A*.

4. Turn this page upside down. Imagine that the graph was scaled in the usual way. Then mark (3, 4). Label it *B*.

5. Turn your page to original position. Follow the grid lines to mark the shortest path between the *B* and *A*.

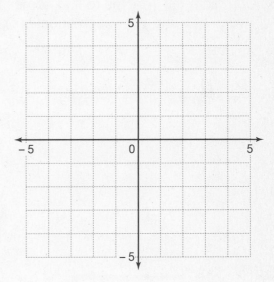

━ Solve ━

6. Does your path go up or down? How many units? _____

7. Does your path go left or right? How many units? _____

━ Look Back ━

8. Are there other paths that you could choose? Explain. _____

_____

9. What is the relationship between the of number of units the path takes and the original coordinates? _____

_____

SOLVE ANOTHER PROBLEM

One item that Norm had to find on a treasure hunt was located at the point (–2, 5) on the map. When Norm got there, he realized he had the map upside down. How many units left, right, up, and down on the map should Norm walk to find the correct location? _____

Graph the equations $y = x + 3$ and $y = x + (-3)$ on the same coordinate plane. Describe the relationship between the lines.

━━ Understand ━━

1. Will you graph the equations on one or two coordinates planes? _____

2. What are you asked to describe? _____

━━ Plan ━━

3. Complete the T-tables to find some values of x and y for each equation.

$y = x + 3$ $y = x + (-3)$

x	y
−1	
0	
1	
2	

x	y
−1	
0	
1	
2	

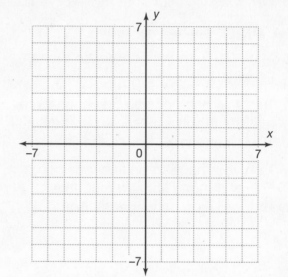

━━ Solve ━━

4. Graph each equation. Label each line.

5. What is the relationship between the lines? _____

_____

━━ Look Back ━━

6. Do you think you would get the same result for the equations $y = x - 3$ and $y = x - (-3)$? Explain. _____

_____

| **SOLVE ANOTHER PROBLEM** |

Graph the equations $y = 3x$ and $y = -3x$ on the coordinate plane above. Label each line. Describe the relationship between the lines.

_____

_____

Name _____

Fire engines carry fire hoses. Fire trucks carry mainly ladders and fire-fighting equipment other than hoses. At one point, the city of San Francisco had 40 fire engines and 18 fire trucks.

  a. Give the ratio of fire engines to fire trucks in lowest terms.

  b. Give the ratio of fire trucks to total fire vehicles in lowest terms.

━ Understand ━

1. How many fire *engines* did the city of San Francisco have? _____

2. How many fire *trucks* did the city of San Francisco have? _____

━ Plan ━

3. How will you find the total number of fire vehicles in San Francisco?

_____

4. What is the total number of fire vehicles in San Francisco? _____

━ Solve ━

5. What is the ratio of fire engines to fire trucks? _____

6. Write your ratio in Item 5 in lowest terms, if possible. _____

7. What is the ratio of fire trucks to total fire vehicles? _____

8. Write your ratio in Item 7 in lowest terms, if possible. _____

━ Look Back ━

9. How can you tell if the ratio is in lowest terms? _____

_____

SOLVE ANOTHER PROBLEM

Use the fire vehicle data above to write each ratio in lowest terms.

  a. What is the ratio of fire trucks to fire engines? _____

  b. What is the ratio of fire vehicles to fire engines? _____

Name _____

The circle graph shows the number of colored beads used in a hand-beaded bracelet. Carole wants to make a smaller bracelet using the same ratios of colors. Draw a circle graph that shows how many beads of each color Carole could use.

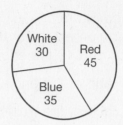

▬ Understand ▬

1. In the circle graph above, how many beads are **a.** white? _____

b. blue? _____ **c.** red? _____ **d.** there in all? _____

▬ Plan ▬

2. Equal ratios can help find the number of beads in the smaller bracelet. Will you multiply or divide to find the equal ratios? _____

3. Write the ratio of blue beads to total beads. Then write an equal ratio. _____ = _____

4. Write each ratio. Then write an equal ratio that has the same number of total beads as the ratio in Item 3.

   a. white beads:total beads _____ **b.** red beads:total beads _____

▬ Solve ▬

5. In the smaller bracelet, how many beads are

   a. there in all? _____ **b.** white? _____

   c. red? _____ **d.** blue? _____

6. Use your answers to Item 5 to draw a circle graph.

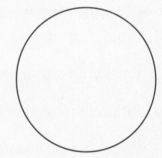

▬ Look Back ▬

7. Did the size of each section in your circle graph change from the size in the graph at the top of the page? Explain. _____

_____

| SOLVE ANOTHER PROBLEM |

Carole wants to make a larger bracelet using the same ratios of colors as in the circle graph at the top of the page. Draw a circle graph that shows how many beads of each color Carole could use.

Name _____

Cameron is making decorations for "Back to School Night." He can make 2 posters in an hour. At this rate, how long will it take him to make 5 posters? Explain.

━━ Understand ━━

1. Circle how many posters Cameron can make in one hour.

2. Underline what you are asked to find.

━━ Plan ━━

3. What is the unit rate to make the posters? _____

4. How many minutes in one hour? _____

5. Write the rate as posters to minutes. _____

6. Complete the table to find an equal rate.

Posters	1		3		5
Minutes		60		120	

━━ Solve ━━

7. How long will it take Cameron to make 5 posters? _____

8. How many *hours* will it take Cameron to make 5 posters? _____

9. Explain how you found your answer. _____

_____

━━ Look Back ━━

10. What is another way to find how long it would take Cameron to make 5 posters? _____

_____

SOLVE ANOTHER PROBLEM

Morgan can make 48 cookies in an hour. At this rate, how long will it take her to make 60 cookies? _____

Janice can run 100 meters in 12 seconds. Carl can run 500 meters in 48 seconds. Susan runs at a rate of 10 meters per second. Phillip can run 200 meters in 24 seconds. Which two students run at the same rate? Explain how you found your answer.

—— Understand ——

1. Underline the question.

2. Write the rate that each student runs in meters per seconds.

   a. Janice _____   **b.** Carl _____   **c.** Susan _____   **d.** Phillip _____

—— Plan ——

3. Make an organized list to compare the pairs of rates.

   a. Janice and Carl _____ $\overset{?}{=}$ _____   **b.** Janice and Susan _____ $\overset{?}{=}$ _____

   c. Janice and Phillip _____ $\overset{?}{=}$ _____   **d.** Carl and Susan _____ $\overset{?}{=}$ _____

   e. Carl and Phillip _____ $\overset{?}{=}$ _____   **f.** Susan and Phillip _____ $\overset{?}{=}$ _____

—— Solve ——

4. Which of the pairs of rates in Item 3 form a proportion? _____

5. Which students run at the same rate? Explain. _____
   _____

—— Look Back ——

6. How could you find which students run at the same rate by writing each rate in lowest terms. _____
   _____

SOLVE ANOTHER PROBLEM

Guillermo made $15 for baby-sitting 5 hours. Megan made $28 in 8 hours. Thomas earned $2.50 in 1 hour, and Della earned $14 in 4 hours. Which two students were paid the same rate? Explain. _____
_____

Darius thought that you could solve proportions only when three of the values are given, and one value is missing. Then he saw the proportion $\frac{4}{x} = \frac{x}{9}$, where two values are given and two are missing. Darius was able to solve the problem. What is the value of *x*? Explain your method.

━━ Understand ━━

1. Write the proportion. _____

2. What are you asked to find? _____

━━ Plan ━━

3. Use the cross products to write an equation. _____

━━ Solve ━━

4. Use mental math to find the value of *x*. _____

5. Explain your method. _____

_____

━━ Look Back ━━

6. What other strategy could you use to find the value of *x*? _____

_____

SOLVE ANOTHER PROBLEM

Lorraine saw the proportion $\frac{x}{x} = \frac{x}{9}$, where one value is given and three are missing. Lorraine was able to solve the problem. What is the value of *x*? How can you use this to give the value of *x* for any similar proportions. Explain.

_____

_____

_____

_____

The *Colossi of Memnon* in Karnak, Egypt, are 21 meters tall. They also measure 70 feet tall. Using these measurements, find the number of meters in a foot.

━━ Understand ━━

1. How tall is the *Colossi of Memnon,* in meters? _____

2. How tall is the *Colossi of Memnon,* in feet? _____

3. It takes more feet than meters to measure the height. Is a meter longer or shorter than a foot? _____

4. What are you asked to find? _____

━━ Plan ━━

5. Write the heights as a ratio of meters to feet. _____

6. Complete the equation to find the unit rate.

$$\frac{\text{meters} \div \rule{1cm}{0.4pt}}{\text{feet} \div \rule{1cm}{0.4pt}} = \frac{\text{meters}}{1 \text{ foot}}$$

━━ Solve ━━

7. Write a sentence giving how many meters are in one foot.

_____

_____

━━ Look Back ━━

8. Let *m* be the number of meters. Use the measurement of the *Colossi* to write a proportion. Then find cross products to solve.

_____

SOLVE ANOTHER PROBLEM

A Jamaican pumpkin soup recipe uses 160 milliliters of light cream. This is equal to 32 teaspoons of light cream. Using these measurements, find the number of milliliters in one teaspoon.   _____

A rectangle has sides of 5 ft and 8 ft. A similar rectangle has two sides of 40 feet. There are two possible answers for the length of the other side of the larger rectangle. What are they?

Understand

1. What are the dimensions of the smaller rectangle? _____

2. What is one dimension of a similar rectangle? _____

3. Underline the number of possible answers.

Plan

4. What is true about matching sides of similar figures? _____

5. Draw the smaller rectangle. Label the sides.

6. Draw another rectangle. Label the sides so that the 40 ft side matches the 5 ft side.

7. Which other side could the 40 ft side match in the smaller rectangle? _____

8. Draw the larger rectangle. Label the sides another way.

Solve

9. Write a proportion to find the missing side of the rectangle drawn

   a. in Item 6. _____   **b.** in Item 8. _____

10. What is the length of the missing side for the rectangle drawn

   a. in Item 6. _____   **b.** in Item 8. _____

Look Back

11. Why did the two sides measuring 40 feet have to be the parallel sides in the rectangle? _____

_____

| SOLVE ANOTHER PROBLEM |

A parallelogram has sides of 2 m and 3 m. A similar parallelogram has two sides of 6 m. There are two possible answers for the length of the other sides of the larger parallelogram. What are they? _____

What percent of the shapes are quadrilaterals?

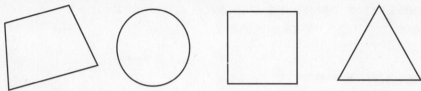

━━ Understand ━━

1. What is the name of the

   a. first figure? _____

   b. second figure? _____

   c. third figure? _____

   d. fourth figure? _____

2. What is the definition of a quadrilateral? _____

━━ Plan ━━

3. Which of the shapes are quadrilaterals? _____

4. Write a ratio of the number of quadrilaterals
   to the total number of figures. _____

5. A percent compares a part to a whole. What
   number represents the whole in a percent? _____

━━ Solve ━━

6. Write an equal ratio to the ratio you wrote in Item 4.
   Use the "whole" you named in Item 5 as the denominator. _____

7. Write the percent of the figures that are quadrilaterals. _____

━━ Look Back ━━

8. What is another way you could find the
   percent of figures that are quadrilaterals?

_____

SOLVE ANOTHER PROBLEM

What percent of the shapes are polygons? _____

If a shirt was originally $20, went on sale for 15% off, and then was
put on clearance with an additional 45% off, estimate the clearance
price of the shirt. Explain your reasoning.

━━ Understand ━━

1. What was the original price of the shirt? _____

2. What was the first discount? _____ The second discount? _____

━━ Plan ━━

3. Is 15% closer to $\frac{1}{10}$, $\frac{2}{10}$, or $\frac{1}{4}$? _____

4. Is 45% closer to $\frac{1}{4}$, $\frac{4}{10}$, or $\frac{1}{2}$? _____

━━ Solve ━━

5. Use the fraction in Item 3 to estimate 15% of $20. _____

6. Subtract the discount to find the first clearance price. _____

7. Use the fraction in Item 4 to estimate 45% of the first clearance price. _____

8. Subtract the discount to find the second clearance price. _____

9. Explain your reasoning. _____

_____

━━ Look Back ━━

10. Do you think your estimated clearance price is
higher or lower than the actual clearance price. Explain. _____

_____

SOLVE ANOTHER PROBLEM

If a jacket was originally $90, went on sale for
30% off, and then was put on clearance with
an additional 15% off, estimate the clearance
price of the jacket. Explain your reasoning. _____

_____

45% of the students at Suburban High School are boys. 30% of the boys at Suburban High School have curly hair. What fraction of the students at Suburban High School are boys with curly hair?

━━ Understand ━━

1. What percent of the students at Suburban High are boys? _____

2. What percent of the boys at Suburban High have curly hair? _____

3. Are you going to write your answer as a percent, a decimal, or a fraction? _____

━━ Plan ━━

4. Suppose you were given the number of boys at Suburban High. How would you find how many boys have curly hair? _____

_____

5. You know the fraction of boys in the school rather than the number of boys. Which operation will you use to find what fraction of students are boys with curly hair? _____

6. Write the number of students that are boys as a fraction. Then rewrite the fraction in lowest terms. _____

7. Write the number of boys that have curly hair as a fraction. Then rewrite the fraction in lowest terms. _____

━━ Solve ━━

8. Write an expression to find the fraction of students that are boys with curly hair. _____

9. What fraction of the students at Suburban High are boys with curly hair? _____

━━ Look Back ━━

10. Show how to estimate to see if your answer is reasonable. _____

_____

SOLVE ANOTHER PROBLEM

20% of the houses on the block are white. 65% of the white houses have blue trim. What fraction of these houses are white with blue trim? _____

© Scott Foresman Addison Wesley 6

A new student's score on a spelling test was about 72% of Catherine's score. Catherine's score was about 98% of Tom's score. Tom's score was about 94% of Luanna's score. Luanna got 93 out of 100 points. How many points did the new student get?

Understand

1. How many points did Luanna score on the spelling test? _____

2. Underline how each student's score relates to another student's score such as, 72% of Catherine's.

Plan

3. Which strategy will you use to find the new student's score? _____

   a. Look for a Pattern   **b.** Draw a Diagram   **c.** Work Backward

4. What operation do you use to find a percent of a number? _____

5. There are no fractional points given for partially correct answers. What should you do if your answer is a decimal? _____

_____

Solve

6. How many points did Tom score? _____

7. How many points did Catherine score? _____

8. How many points did the new student score? _____

Look Back

9. Order the students scores from least to greatest. Does this correspond with the clues given in the problem? _____

_____

SOLVE ANOTHER PROBLEM

Eden's bowling score was about 96% of Remy's score. Remy's score was about 75% of Laneesha's score. Laneesha's score was 100% of Martin's score. Martin's bowling score was 150 points. How many points did the Eden score? _____

Name _____

Use what you know about triangular, rectangular, and pentagonal prisms to draw a hexagonal prism. Classify each of the faces and explain your drawing.

━ Understand ━

1. What are you asked to draw? _____

2. Does a prism have one base or two parallel, congruent bases? _____

━ Plan ━

3. What polygon makes up the base for each of these prisms?

a. Triangular _____   **b.** Rectangular _____

c. Pentagonal _____

4. What polygon will make up the base of a hexagonal prism? _____

5. What polygon makes up the sides for each of the three given prisms? _____

6. What polygon will make up the sides of a hexagonal prism? _____

━ Solve ━

7. Draw a hexagonal prism.

8. Explain your drawing.

_____

━ Look Back ━

9. What is the pattern in the number of faces in triangular, rectangular, and pentagonal prisms? How many faces will be in a hexagonal prism?

_____

_____

SOLVE ANOTHER PROBLEM

Draw an octagonal prism. Classify each of the faces and explain your drawing?

_____

Name _____

If wrapping paper costs $0.29 a square
foot, how much would it cost to cover the
box shown?

1 ft.

0.3 ft.   1 ft.

━━ Understand ━━

1. Underline what you are asked to find.

2. How much does the wrapping paper cost? _____

━━ Plan ━━

3. How many faces does the box have? _____

4. What shape is each face? _____

5. Which net can you use to make the box? _____

a.

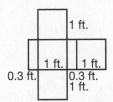

1 ft.

1 ft.   1 ft.

0.3 ft.   0.3 ft.
1 ft.

b.   0.3 ft.

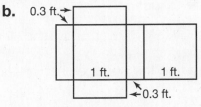

1 ft.   1 ft.

0.3 ft.

6. Find the area of the top and bottom faces. 2 × ____ × ____ = ____

7. Find the area of the front and back faces. 2 × ____ × ____ = ____

8. Find the area of the left and right faces. 2 × ____ × ____ = ____

9. What is the surface area of the box? _____

━━ Solve ━━

10. Multiply to find the cost of the paper needed
to cover the box without overlapping edges. _____

━━ Look Back ━━

11. Could you draw a different net for the box? Would it change your answer? Explain.

_____

SOLVE ANOTHER PROBLEM

If wrapping paper costs $2.50 a square meter,
how much would it cost to cover the box shown? _____

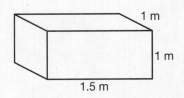

1 m

1 m

1.5 m

Name _____

Which solid has the greater surface area? Explain.

a.

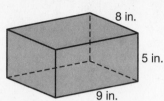

8 in.

5 in.

9 in.

b.

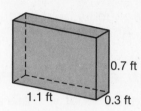

0.7 ft

1.1 ft

0.3 ft

Understand

1. What are you asked to compare? _____

2. Are the units of measurement the same or different in each solid? _____

Plan

3. How can you convert feet to inches? _____

4. Convert each measure to inches.

   a. 1.1 ft _____   **b.** 0.7 ft _____   **c.** 0.3 ft _____

5. What is the formula to find the surface area of each solid? ____

   a. $SA = (2 \times l \times w) + (2 \times l \times h) + (2 \times w \times h)$ **b.** $SA = s^2$

Solve

6. What is the surface area in square inches of Solid a? _____

7. What is the surface area in square inches of Solid b? _____

8. Which solid has the greater surface area? Explain.

_____

Look Back

9. How could you find the answer in another way? _____

_____

SOLVE ANOTHER PROBLEM

Which solid has the greater surface area? Explain.

a.

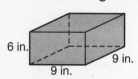

6 in.

9 in.

9 in.

b.

0.5 ft

0.9 ft

0.7 ft

_____

A can of cake frosting is 4.5 inches tall and has a 3 inch diameter.

    a. If there is no overlap, what is the area of the can's label?

    b. What is the surface area of the entire can?

═ Understand ═

1. Underline the height and diameter of the can.

2. Does the side or the base of a can contain the label? _____

═ Plan ═

3. What shape is the side of a cylinder? _____

4. What is the formula to find the area of the side of a cylinder? ___

    a. $A = 2\pi r^2$ **b.** $A = h \times 2\pi r$ **c.** $A = d\pi$

5. What shape is the base of a cylinder? _____

6. What is the formula to find the area of the base of a cylinder? _____

7. How can you find the total surface area of the can once you know the areas of the base and the side? _____

8. What is the radius of the can? _____

═ Solve ═

9. What is the area of the can's label? _____

10. What is the surface area of the entire can? _____

═ Look Back ═

11. Write the surface area formula. Then use it to check your answer to Item 10.

_____

SOLVE ANOTHER PROBLEM

A can is 6.5 inches tall and has a 5 inch diameter.

    a. If there is no overlap, what is the area of the can's label? _____

    b. What is the surface area of the entire can? _____

Name _____

Describe the pattern.
How many cubes are in the
eighth solid of the pattern?

  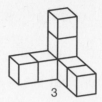

━━ Understand ━━

1. You are asked to find the number of cubes in which place in the pattern? _____

━━ Plan ━━

2. Count the cubes in each figure in the pattern and use this data to complete the table.

Place	1	2	3				
Number of Cubes							

━━ Solve ━━

3. What is the rule for the pattern? _____

4. Describe the pattern. Include how each figure in the pattern physically changes.

_____

_____

5. How many cubes are in the eighth solid of the pattern? _____

━━ Look Back ━━

6. Continue the table to check your answer. What other strategy could you use to check your answer?

_____

┌─────────────────────────────┐
│   **SOLVE ANOTHER PROBLEM**   │
└─────────────────────────────┘

Describe the pattern.
How many cubes are in the tenth solid
of the pattern?

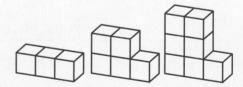

_____

Name _____

When sugar cubes are produced, they are put into tightly packed boxes for purchasing. If the box of sugar cubes shown is 3 cubes high, how many sugar cubes are in the box?

━━ Understand ━━

1. How many sugar cubes high is the box? _____

2. What are you asked to find? _____

━━ Plan ━━

3. How many cubes are in one row? _____

4. How many cubes are in one column? _____

5. How many cubes are in one layer? _____

━━ Solve ━━

6. Complete the number sentence to find the number of sugar cubes in the box. ____ × ____ = _____

7. Write a sentence giving the number of cubes in the box. _____

_____

━━ Look Back ━━

8. Draw a diagram of each layer of sugar cubes. Make sure that the number of cubes matches your answer to Item 6.

SOLVE ANOTHER PROBLEM

Centimeter cubes can be placed in tightly packed boxes. If the box of centimeter cubes shown is 4 cubes high, how many centimeter cubes are in the box?

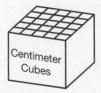

Centimeter Cubes

_____

The volume of a gallon of water is about 231 cubic inches.
If a 25-gallon aquarium is 32 inches long and 15 inches wide,
how deep is it? Explain.

—— Understand ——

1. What are you asked to find? _____

2. What is the volume of a gallon of water? _____

3. Underline the dimensions of the aquarium that are given.

—— Plan ——

4. How can you find the volume of an
   aquarium that holds 25 gallons of water? _____

5. What is the volume of the aquarium? _____

6. What is the formula to find the volume of a rectangular prism?

   _____

7. Substitute known values into the equation you wrote in Item 6.

   _____

—— Solve ——

8. Multiply values in the equation. _____

9. Use mental math, or guess and check to find
   the depth of the aquarium to the nearest whole number. _____

10. How deep is the aquarium? Explain. _____

    _____

—— Look Back ——

11. Estimate to see if your answer is reasonable. _____

    _____

| SOLVE ANOTHER PROBLEM |

The volume of a gallon of water is about 231 cubic inches. If a 30-gallon
aquarium is 25 inches long and 25 inches wide, how deep is it? Explain.

_____

Name _____

Suppose you roll a number cube. Find P(even number).

━ Understand ━

1. What does the problem ask you to find?

_____

━ Plan ━

2. How many numbers are on a number cube? _____

3. How many possible outcomes are there when you roll a number cube? _____

4. What are the even numbers on a number cube? _____

5. How many ways can you roll an even number? _____

━ Solve ━

6. Write the probability of rolling an even number. Which ratio will you use? _____

a. $P(\text{event}) = \dfrac{\text{number of ways event can happen}}{\text{number of possible outcomes}}$

b. $P(\text{event}) = \dfrac{\text{number of possible outcomes}}{\text{number of ways event can happen}}$

7. Write the probability. _____

━ Look Back ━

7. Are all the possible outcomes equally likely? How do you know?

_____

| SOLVE ANOTHER PROBLEM |

Suppose you toss a twelve-sided number cube with numbers 1-12 on its faces. What is the probability of rolling a number which is a multiple of 5?

_____

Hurricane season in the United States is from June 1 to November 30. In an average season, there are ten tropical storms. Six are expected to reach hurricane strength and two of these are likely to strike the U.S. coast.

Is the probability that a tropical storm will turn into a hurricane more than 50%?

▬ Understand ▬

1. How many tropical storms are there in an average season? _____

2. How many of the tropical storms are expected
to reach hurricane strength in an average season? _____

▬ Plan ▬

3. Describe the ratio you will use to show the probability that a
tropical storm will turn into a hurricane.

_____

_____

4. What will you compare the ratio to? _____

▬ Solve ▬

5. Find the probability that a tropical storm will turn into a hurricane. _____

6. Write the probability as a percent. _____

7. Is the percentage less than, equal to, or greater than 50%? _____

▬ Look Back ▬

8. How could you answer the question without changing the
probability to a percent?

_____

_____

SOLVE ANOTHER PROBLEM

Suppose 20 tropical storms are predicted.
Twelve are expected to reach hurricane strength.
What percentage will probably *not* become hurricanes? _____

Hurricanes blow in a spiral around a circular center known as the
"eye." If a storm covers a circular area 400 miles wide and its eye is
20 miles wide, what is the probability of an object in a hurricane being
in the eye of the hurricane?

━━ Understand ━━

1. What is the width of the hurricane? _____

2. What is the width of the hurricane's eye? _____

3. What shape is the hurricane? The hurricane's eye? _____

━━ Plan ━━

4. Which ratio will you use to find the probability
   of an object being in the eye of the hurricane? _____

   a. $\dfrac{\text{Area of the eye}}{\text{Area of the hurricane}}$

   b. $\dfrac{\text{Area of the hurricane}}{\text{Area of the eye}}$

5. Which formula will you use to find the area of the hurricane and of its eye? _____

   a. $A = Bh$ b. $A = s^2$ c. $A = \pi r^2$

━━ Solve ━━

6. What is the area of the hurricane? _____

7. What is the area of the eye of the hurricane? _____

8. What is the probability of an object being in the eye of the hurricane?

   _____

━━ Look Back ━━

9. How can you Solve a Simpler Problem to see if your answer is reasonable?

   _____

   _____

SOLVE ANOTHER PROBLEM

What is the probability of an object being
in the eye of a hurricane if the hurricane is
600 miles wide and its eye is 40 miles wide? _____

The lunch choices of the day are bologna or peanut butter sandwich
with either an apple, orange, or banana, and either juice or milk. Draw
a tree diagram showing all possible outcomes.

▬ Understand ▬

1. What are you asked to draw? _____

2. What will you show on your drawing? _____

▬ Plan ▬

3. Which lunch choice will you list

   a. first? _____ **b.** second? _____ **c.** third? _____

▬ Solve ▬

4. Make a tree diagram by listing your first lunch choice and drawing lines
   to your second and third choices. Then list all possible choices.

   Sandwiches   **Fruits**   **Drinks**   **Possible choices**

▬ Look Back ▬

5. How can you check to see if your answer is reasonable?

_____

SOLVE ANOTHER PROBLEM

How many possible choices would there be if soda was also
available? You can draw a diagram on another sheet of paper to help you. _____

Name _____

The probability of a newborn child being a girl is about $\frac{1}{2}$. What is the probability of all 5 children in a family being girls?

━━ Understand ━━

1. What is the probability of a newborn child being a girl? _____

2. What are you asked to find?

_____

━━ Plan ━━

3. What is the outcome? _____

   a. Gender of the child   **b.** Number of children in family

4. How many possible outcomes are there for each event? _____

5. How many of the possible outcomes normally will be girls? _____

6. How many events are there? _____

━━ Solve ━━

7. Multiply to find the total number of possible outcomes for all events.

   _____ × _____ × _____ × _____ × _____ = _____

8. Multiply to find the number of possible outcomes that result in the birth of a girl for all events.

   _____ × _____ × _____ × _____ × _____ = _____

9. What is the probability of all 5 children in a family being girls as a ratio? _____

━━ Look Back ━━

10. Since the probability given was *about* $\frac{1}{2}$, will your final answer be exact or approximate?

_____

| SOLVE ANOTHER PROBLEM |

What is the probability of all 4 children in a family being boys? _____

Name _____

Determine if the game is fair. If it is *not*, tell which player has the higher probability of winning.

A nickel and a dime are tossed. The winner is determined as shown.

Tim wins   Vern wins   Maggie wins   Urse wins

▬ Understand ▬

1. How many possible outcomes are there when the coins are tossed? _____

2. How many possible outcomes are the same? _____

▬ Plan ▬

3. What is the probability that Tim will win? _____

4. What is the probability that Maggie will win? _____

5. What is the probability that Vern will win? _____

6. What is the probability that Urse will win? _____

▬ Solve ▬

7. Is the game fair or unfair? Explain.

_____

▬ Look Back ▬

8. Both Tim's and Vern's coins show a head and a tail? How do they differ?

_____

| SOLVE ANOTHER PROBLEM |

Suppose Tim, Vern, and Urse toss two nickels. Tim wins if two tails are tossed. Vern wins if two heads are tossed. Urse wins if a head and a tail are tossed. Is the game fair or unfair? Explain.

_____

_____